Alice O'g

A novel by Clara Devine

©Clara Devine 2024

First Published 2024 in association with

Geraldine Granleese Books

and

Feeny Community Association

Clara Devine

This is a work of fiction. Any resemblance to actual persons, living or dead, or actual events is purely coincidental

Chapter 1

My name is Alice Oakgrove and I was born on the 26th of March 1863. I would say my life is quite plain but what's about to happen is not so plain. When I was an infant I grew up in the country-side, so my life was quite peaceful the first few years of my life, though when I turned seven things began to change.

Growing up we had a housemaid called Anne. She was an elegant and gentle person and always got our things for us quite quickly but carefully. She had black curly hair with bright green eyes I loved her so dearly as she was like a second mother to me, but her mother had tragically passed away, she had to leave our home and go back to Denmark where she was from. When she left I cried and cried and promised her I would never forget her.

Life was not the same without her but now we move on to me. I have wavy curly pale brown hair with wonderfully hazel brown eyes with tan skin. I am quite a good person. I would like to say, I was never that timid but when or if I was my big brother Fred was there to stand up for me. Fred has dark ginger taking after father he was quite tall for being fifteen years of age.

So when I turned eight we got a new housemaid who was called Martha. She never was nice and was always nudging me to stop doing something just for the fun of it. She also liked poking me and she would never, ever, ever read to me at bedtime. So when Father and Mother declared they were leaving to go on a trip to Ireland for the 50th celebration for my Grandads farm being open they said they were leaving for 8 months.my first instinct was to get excited to go to Ireland because I had never been, when they said it was only them going I was devastated they said "sorry honey it is only me and your father going, you nor Fred is going but Martha will kindly look after you and Fred for the time period we are gone"

Finally it was time for Mother and Father to leave I cried and said I wanted to go with them but they refused and dragged me from them then they kissed me goodbye and went and hopped in the carriage and then they left, me and Fred waved and waved until they were the size of a dot and we looked up at Martha's stubby little face she had a sinister smile on it as it was only mid-morning we gulped we had a day full of work waiting for us. We spent the rest of the day being obedient to Martha following her rules around the house she was ordering us about do this do that. She made me do the washing clean all our plates from past meals, when I was upstairs sorting out frocks and dresses and putting dirty ones in a basket to clean Martha came up and reminded me to make her frock and shawl I wish she had forgotten about that as I was expected to do it perfectly because I was trained for 4 years on how to do it, so my hands were really neat and nimble and you could barely see anywhere where I patched up or sewed. I was getting sick of her ordering me about so I literally lost it and screamed at her " OH WOW HAVE YOU EVER DID THIS? I DIDN'T THINK SO YOU'RE THE WORST HOUSEMAID EVER YOU'RE NOT EVEN A HOUSEMAID IF YOU WERE THEN YOU WOULD ACTUALLY DO THIS BUT NO YOU'RE FAR TOO LAZY TO

DO THIS YOU'RE MEANT TO LOOK AFTER US HERE AND IT'S THE OTHER WAY ABOUT AT THE MOMENT!!!!!!!!!!!" I panted the last few words as I struggled for breath. Fred had heard me and didn't want me to get in trouble so he dramatically started apologizing that I go wild sometimes and didn't mean any of that but OH I meant every bit of it. Martha had heard me okay but she didn't start raging like she usually did she kept her cool controlled. I noticed a gleam in her eye as she looked upwards she suddenly grabbed my thin delicate wrist and I winced in pain as she tightened her rough grip on my arm she dragged me to the stairs and started climbing onwards and upwards OH NO! I thought not the attic.

Chapter 2

The attic is an old space in our house, it is up at the highest point in our house it is filled with a whole load of old junk for example old broken dolls, an old musty crusty dusty disgusting old chamber pot from earlier times when other people were here as servants, teddy bears with stuffing off of them and big rips and heaps of old clothes from when we were infants and clothes that are ripped or just too terrible to wear anymore.

It was not very spacious I'll tell you that with everything in it but there was just a small space about 90 centimetres so not a lot. As Martha led me up spiral staircases after staircases I felt dizzy not because my hand and wrist were almost white and purple from Martha gripping so tightly it was because the stairs were uneven and were easy to slip and fall on. I did multiple times but nothing happened. I was just dragged along by Martha.

Once we were up at the top of the house Martha opened a series of locks on the unstable brown door I did not trust it to lean against as I was gazing at it. Martha had finally opened the locks I forgot about being took in here I was focused on the pain of my wrist and the door I started kicking and screaming my head off really viciously but she was to big and strong she just thrust me in the attic and bolted the door again while I Was left there kicking and screaming "that'll put some sense into silly little feisty Alice" she murmured just loud enough for me to hear "I heard that!!!!!!" I screamed as she left cackling away to herself. I still pounded on the door my hands became more bloody, cut and sore so I stopped, accepting that she wasn't coming back. I decided if I was stuck up here I might as well explore up here I Looked around and seen my old dolls I used to play with now all battered and broken I knew the sun was setting so I felt my way past the teddy bears to the old clothes I found an old blanket and pillow so I set up there and I attempted to sleep, I failed miserably but I felt the eerily sound of quietness scary but I also heard the swaying of the trees in the light breeze soothing I eventually rested and dreamt about me and my brother playing up in the clouds and I dozed off immediately.

In the morning I woke bright and early to the sound of my stomach rumbling. It was only then that I remembered that I was locked up. I was up there alone for so long I didn't know if I was hallucinating or if there were soft snores on the other side of the door so I gently tapped the wooden door and the person on the other side awoke immediately and said "is that Alice?" I first thought Martha slept there and waited for me but no she seemed too cruel for that and also this voice seemed raspy and familiar. It was Fred. "Yes, it's Alice." "Okay so I stole the keys to this room but the door doesn't look too pleasant but I'll try opening it up so you can get out, but you will have to hide from Martha because she's planning to leave you up there until mother and father come back" "but that's another 7 months away" I said "eight" Fred corrected me. That was horrible, from the other side of the door Fred scrambled about making noises so loud trying to open the locks "sssssssssssssssssssssshhhhhhhhhhhhhhhhhhhhhhhhh" I whisper shouted.

Now desperately hungry I searched around for some food or liquid, I found an old can of bacon half opened and suddenly ravenous ,I ate desperately for some energy. I did not care for the taste at all because it tasted like jerky but it gave me energy and it helped. Fred tried endlessly trying to open the locks up when at last it popped open and the door creakily made its way open and I got excited silently and ran to Fred to give him a hug.

We quickly made our way down to make sure Martha didn't notice Fred was gone for a while but then suddenly my body jerked in the wrong direction as I went down the staircase and I tripped on the uneven stairs and went tumbling down, down, down it was like I was falling down a big black hole continually on end.

Chapter 3

My body regained consciousness after a while. I was horrified to be looking straight into the eyes of………Martha? She gave me a disapproving look and I felt the itchiness of a dirty rough mattress. I glanced to the right to see Fred's face pale white as if he was one ghost whiter than ever turn back to normal colour as he flung his arms around me "I thought we lost you there, oh the pain you must be experiencing right now must be excruciating that was a bad fall you took there.

I was shook all over when it happened and you looked so lifeless" he exclaimed all at once as if he was the only boy on earth who cared about anything. " Well my head doesn't hurt that bad but I suppose that my arms and chest hurt quite a bit" I said quite casually though the pain was making me exhausted thinking about it I still was a bit whoozy but I managed to steady myself before I fell "Oh alright that's enough chatting about it. It happened , it's done, it's in the past now forget about it" "if you are not going to obey these rules that I make you will not make me pleased so scram Alice I'd rather split you up than you together and also Fred is good company and is a rule follower, Alice you are a spiteful little creature and a screeching banshee now be off with you in the morning" then she laughed again even more sinister than her smile it was clear she practiced that many times before.

I just stood there silenced and astonished by her words whizzing around my head suddenly filled with millions of different questions. "That's right scram!" she said it more sternly now. I sat up in my room while my head buzzed around frantically wanting to know the answers to them all. My head was like this: okay what will we do to stay here? If we get kicked out what will happen? I need to make a living. How will I make a living? Where will I live? What if I don't have a house? Why has this happened?: my palms turned sweaty and my fists were clenched. My head turned all fuzzy and my eyes dropped tears.

I couldn't get out of these thoughts. My eyes did not want the waterworks to stop so now uncontrollably I was shaking. Fred came in to calm me down and told me to stop fretting and breathe deep. I did as I was told and took breaths in and out. I calmed down and he stepped into the action. Fred said he had a plan and we were leaving to go on the streets to live somewhere else until mother and father came back and then come back weeping and blame Martha for everything and then she will get kicked out of the house and we will live happily ever after the end so I started to pack but I soon realised that I did not have very much stuff to pack all I had was multiple dresses and frocks and some stockings, a doll that I named Rosemary but I once was playing with her outside one summer and I went inside for lunch, when I came out she melted slightly with the warmth of the sun it was only a little melt but I was devastated and destroyed the purpose of her, a violet bow and some pieces of a jigsaw puzzle I packed them neatly in a bag of neatly embroidered flowers with my one and only shawl.

Chapter 4

I felt a surge of excitement rush through me as I was leaving home for the first time in forever but I also felt a pang of guilt as I was disobeying the rules of my parents to not leave the house. They will be petrified when they come back and I'm not there they would call the police to find us and bring us to safety. I got sucked away in a world of scenarios that I didn't notice Fred calling me to get my night clothes on so when I did I put on my silk night robe and cleaned my teeth and hopped into my bed and I slept rather well as I was in the attic the night before so it was nice to have a soft mattress to lie on.

I woke up in the middle of the night wailing because I had a nightmare but mother wasn't there to cradle me and father wasn't there to sing me silly songs. I woke up less than 2 hours later and could not get back to sleep no matter how exhausted I was I stayed up. I slipped out of the house even though it was quite dark and breezy. I wrapped myself up in my shawl, tightly. I was chanting my street name over and over in case I forgot and got lost.

I was so busy chanting my street name that I saw the name Fairfield Avenue as I passed and it was quite close to my street so I memorized that instead it was quite busy for it being quite early in the morning but people were going about everywhere asking for directions I was cautious when I was walking and kept out of the road of suspicious people as I had 4 shillings in my pocket for food and a drink, I asked a kindly man if he knew any food stalls nearby and he sniggered and replied "just follow your boots missus" he cackled at this and passers-by sniggered at this I felt my cheeks burning with humiliation and huffed on but when I had my head down I lost all sense of direction and I lost my shillings, when I asked multiple children and adults none of them new where Fairfield avenue was they were clueless I lost all hope and panic spread all over me rushing through each part of my body.

I crouched down on the sidewalk and just sat there shivering. I zoned out the world and just focused on myself. Just then I heard a clink on the stone hard pavement and I looked up to see a little old lady smiling down at me as she dropped a penny at my feet she walked on and I picked it up and gazed at it, it was shiny and had a bronze glow. I soon realized because I was so short and tiny people would have sympathy for me and drop pennies so I did that rather a lot even though I didn't have to.

Once I had got a handful of pennies at least worth one shilling or more I got up wrapped my money in my shawl and walked on my way I seen a little girl with her maid and she and her maid looked so happy together so I dared to approach them and they welcomed me and I asked politely "excuse me do you happen to know where any food stalls are nearby" "yes of course darling you look like you could do with some eating you're so small what age are you?" she asked. "I am seven years old, turning eight in March" I said. "Well there is a place called the Dough Drop run by a girl called Margaret though she's quite old, her bakery is homemade and delicious" "isn't it Rosabelle" "oh yes, yes it is very nice" said Rosabelle. Rosabelle had soft blonde hair in nice neat plaits with pink bows tied to the ends of her hair. She wore a velvet light mauve and white lace dress with embroidered strawberries on the top of the bodice. She looked at least 8 or 9 and was very shy but nice.

"Thank you very much" I said, thankful as I was getting hungry. "But could you please give me directions on where to go? I'm not from around here" I asked again. "Of course their bakery is just left from here and then just simply right and the third stall on the right hand side of the road." "bye" I said "goodbye" her and Rosabelle chorused. I followed their directions and soon enough found the Dough Drop and I went inside it was humongous it had a whole big stall for cakes and one for cupcakes and even one for pretzels it looked delicious and the smell was wafting all around I got in a queue with about seven other people and waited and looked for what I would want and I see this vanilla cupcake with pink and lilac sprinkles it also had light baby pink frills on the outer bit of it. It was so pretty and I had just enough for it.

As I got further up the queue I was so excited to try it and Margaret seemed nice she was having little conversations with "daily customers" and her hair was up in a net so it didn't go in the food. When it came to my turn she said "hello missus I have not seen you before are you a traveller?" "yes I'm not from here" "well anyway what would you like" she said. "Well this is my first time here but there is one thing that I would like, it is the pink and purple cupcake" I said happy that no one had taken it. "Of course my dear, that will be two shillings," she said. I gave her all my coins and she counted them up and said "you are one penny short so you cannot get it" my heart dropped but then she roared with laughter "only pulling your leg child, your face!"

She wiped her eyes and handed me the cupcake and 4 pennies back. "Thank you so much" I said trying to cover up my embarrassment and I hurried out I sat on the bench of the park I met the maid and Rosabelle and ate on my first bite it was so creamy and good my mouth was melting eating it, it crumbled right off satisfyingly and when I finished I asked the lady on the next bench if she knew where Fairfield was and she said to just follow the right and then take a sharp left and then you cut on to Curtinvale Road and keep walking straight and then you are there so I thanked her and went on my way but when I turned the sharp left I panicked because I forgot where to go next but then I saw the sign Curtinvale Road and kept walking straight.

I finally got to Fairfield and then I found my street Synaparth Park and I got to my house number 213. I slipped in as easy as I slipped out as they were just waking up. Fred was planning to disappear with me before Martha wakes up fully and goes downstairs and sees so Fred was just downstairs getting everything in his bag. I went up, grabbed my suitcase with everything in it and we said farewell to our home because we won't be in it for a while and then we were off.

Chapter 5

First of all on our journey Fred had no idea where we were going but I suggested that we go to the park but Fred said "you have got to stop with your imagination there's no such things this is reality not kid play" "no but this is real I seen it today when I went out an hour ago! It's just past Fairfield Avenue and it is wonderful" I exclaimed. "Okay then if you insist take me go on" Fred sneered.

I wondered why he was so mean all of a sudden but he was kidding. So I walked straight and in the distance I saw the name Fairfield Avenue and I went to the left and seen Curtinvale Road and then turned right and we were there the park and it had a sign that I had not seen earlier but it read, Welcome to Evergreen Park! We are one of England's most beautiful parks for Autumn leaves with multi colours. We have the cleanest lake and have had for a long time. Please enjoy and don't feed our ducks any more than two slices of bread each thank you. It was bordered with little ducks swimming.

We walked in the park and sat down on a nearby bench and rested then Fred handed me 4 shillings and said to go spend it at the shops and he also said I was to explore more and that he wants to rest so I can go have fun. But he also said that to be careful because there is people that take people's money. So he sent me on my way and I went and roamed the stalls and I was tempted to get another dessert from the Dough Drop but then it seemed rude going in twice in a row so I went to the stalls instead, I eyed this spiral fountain pen with a little feather at the top with little swirly patterns around it I wanted it but I also wanted to spend something on Fred so I got the fountain pen and I looked for Fred but it seemed impossible to know what he likes so I ended up getting the pen and a leathery gold notebook with my name on it and a new pair of shoes for him as his shoes are rather broken so I had about three pennies left after that but I wanted to go to the Dough Drop and let Fred try it to see if he likes it and let me go back. So I went to the Dough Drop and waited in queue and when I got to the top of the line Margaret said "well fancy seeing you back what can I get you? Again ""ummm well do you have anything you could get me for" I counted up the pennies "three pennies?" I asked. "Of course I do. What do you fancy, a pretzel or a small cookie?" Well do you have a couple pretzels? It's not for me it's for my brother and could you bag it up please I have to walk quite far" I said politely. "Well I could give you ten pretzels for five pennies but you only have four but I'll let you off as you are so little and slight and I'll bag that up for you too does that sound to you like your perfection missy?" she said trying not to laugh

"Of course it does," I said, amazed that I'm starting to like her a lot. "I'm thinking about promoting you to daily customers if you plan to show up again. See you around?" she said. "Of course, well if my brother approves we ran away so I thought I would come to your bakery as it's the nicest around in town" I said hopeful she would add another couple pretzels and to my surprise she did. "A little more treats for your runner goodbye miss..." "you can just call me Alice" I blurted out. "Okey dokey now you run along before I spank you with my tea towel!" Then she cackled again but I didn't chance it. I grabbed the bag and dropped the pennies on the counter and darted out the door.

I wrapped everything up in my shawl and hurried up to the park as it was mid-afternoon and I wanted lunch. I showed the stuff to Fred and he said all the money was for me not for him but he was happy otherwise. But he was even more shocked when I showed him new boots and he was so overjoyed "thank you so much! I have wanted these for a while but I couldn't get them!" "I'm glad you like them but look what I got!" I showed him my new fountain pen and the leathery gold notebook and he was amazed "made for a princess" he exclaimed.

We got out the pretzels and I started munching on them but soon followed by Fred saying "hey leave some for me you little munchkin!" he said and that also included tipping me upside down and shaking me. I was almost in tears laughing when he finished. So when we finished the pretzels I opened up my gold notebook to the first page and it looked very scratchy and when I got out my fountain pen I thought about what to draw when I decided that I was going to be a landscape of the park I got my first line and it was distractingly scratchy so some bits of my drawing was blotchy but it didn't matter because drawing was going beautifully when I finished it was just about evening.

It was a lot colder now than earlier so me and Fred went to look for shelter so we went to stand underneath a fish stall but it was stinking of fish so we went into a tea shop but the woman there said that we could not stay unless we bought a drink so we had to buy a cup of tea and we took it in turns taking sips we spent as long as we could so we did not have to go back outside but the lady caught on and shooed us away so we scurried out but it had warmed up slightly we got our cases and sat on the bench soon Fred said we had to go on with our journey but first Fred had to use the lavatory so he left to go find one so he said for me to wait on the bench so I did as I was told and waited and waited but I got bored so I got out my book and started to draw a moon coming out of the clouds but I did not notice that happening in real life I got panicked because I know no one takes that long in the lavatory I grabbed my belongings and wandered off I longed for him to come back but he did not.

Chapter 6

I found this shop which was closed down, maybe abandoned so I set up there with my stuff near me. I tried to go to sleep but it was still quite busy on the streets so it was hard to go to sleep but my eyes soon drooped and I dozed off. I thought about what would happen if I went back to Martha but that would not end well. There was lots more noise soon after I fell asleep. When I woke up I woke up to the sound of footsteps I first noticed that ALL of my belongings were gone, heartbroken I went and searched for them I only found my rosemary doll in the shop but that was it.

When I was walking I cut down a dark alleyway and I see two gleaming eyes staring straight at me. I screamed but they clamped their hands over my mouth "sssssssssssshhhhhhhhhhhhhhh" she whispered. "You're gonna scare my hamster whiskers!" "Who are you?" I hissed. "I am.... Well I've never actually had an actual name but you can call me ..." her voice trailed off "I'll call you Victoria" I said though that name seemed too grand for this voice to suit but still. "I'm not complaining," said Victoria. "Why are you here?" "Well I already told you I'm looking for my hamster whiskers!"

Just then I felt warm soft fur swish over my foot. "I think he is here" and I picked him up. We went out to the daylight and I gave her whiskers but she actually did look like a Victoria. She had light pale strawberry blonde hair and had an old tattered dress but she still managed to look astonishing and just something about her made her more distinctive than others. "Thank you" she said "you know I never asked your name what's yours?" "uumm well I am Alice and my birthday is March Twenty Sixth Eighteen Sixty Three. What about yours?" "my birthday is March Twenty Sixth Eighteen Sixty Three!" "we have the same birthday!!" We both said at the same time.

Then Victoria asked where my parents were so I told her about them going on a trip to Ireland to my Grandad's farm. I asked about hers but she said that her family used to live in a big house but then her father lost his job and then they became poor and then her parents went to a party but then they just disappeared. (keep in mind this is her version of the story) So she went out to the street but an old nanny came and asked where her parents were but she said they were lost so the nanny took her to the orphanage, she lived there for a while but it was horrid so she tried to escape multiple times but she was caught and spanked for her despicable behaviour.

She chanced it one more time in the dead of night and escaped without getting caught! Then she slept on a bench and then woke up and went for a walk but whiskers got lost down that alleyway so she went down there and then she saw me!! Her life is much more exciting than mine. So I told her about being a servant to a maid and being locked up in the attic for one and a half days and she was amazed. I asked her if she wanted to go to the park called Evergreen Park but she declined and said we should go to the park near there about half a mile away called Frecknal Park so I said yes because I wanted to explore so we went there. It was not far from Curtinvale Road; just in the other direction of it so we went to there and it was beautiful as well because it had an enormous lake far bigger than the one in Evergreen Park also it was quite hilly so you could sit down at an angle.

Victoria wanted to go paddle as it was a hotter day than yesterday so she went to the lake and I perched myself on the grassy hill and played with Rosemary (also I found my pen and notebook in the dark alleyway) and I took out my book and fountain pen and showed them to Rosemary and I made her look shocked I decided to draw a picture of Victoria swimming but all to soon she was out with her clothes back on and she was telling me to come on and she was hungry. I told her we didn't have any money but she had a shilling or two so I told her it was my turn to pick where we went so I chose the Dough Drop. I feel like I have been going there too much lately but that could not be helped. So we approached the Dough Drop after a long time of complaining.

Obviously Victoria did it all but when we approached it she started gazing at all of the bakeries windows. We stepped in line and Victoria wanted everything but she ended up deciding on this chocolate cookie that I agreed with and it looked delicious. We got up in front of the line and Margaret exclaimed "seriously how many times have you been here in the past two days?!" I blushed at this "three times" I said in a muffled voice. "Who is this you have with you now, your sister?" "No, actually she is my friend called Victoria" I replied. "Okay okay what can I get you?" "And Victoria," I pointed out. "Anyway we would like a chocolate cookie over there" and Victoria pointed. "Oh yes only one left, it is very popular. "Margaret?" "yes my dear" " do you happen to know a maid with a little girl that comes here called

Rosabelle?" I asked. "Oh yes I am her grandma she is a little charm isn't she"

Taken aback I was shocked. "How do you know them?" Margaret exclaimed. "Well they were the ones that encouraged me to go here in the first place" "oh yes there would be no other bakeries they would point out to people, bless them, where is your brother, did he do a runner on you?" "oh no I was waiting for him to come back to me from the lavatory but he never did so then I met Victoria!" "oh well good luck on your journey" she called as we paid and walked out. We shared the cookie and split it in half even though I purposely let Victoria get the slightly bigger piece. "Mmmmm this is delicious we have got to go back, anyway what is that I hear about Rosabed or whatever her name was?" "Rosabelle" I corrected her.

Chapter 7

It was getting darker now, the sun was setting so we looked about for a place to sleep but we found a really hollow tree and it was very thick so there was a lot of space, more than the attic in my house. We squeezed in and then we set up for the night, we found this really big log though it was flat but that was a good thing so we dragged it and placed it at the side of the tree like a door and then we found some string so we really did fashion it into a door we had some leftover string so we tied it to the back of the door so from the inside you could pull it shut it was amazing.

Victoria went and left to go get leaves for a blanket but even better she came back with an old blanket and it was fluffy and I also had my shawl and I used that as a pillow for me and her. It was very comfy for being in a tree; we chatted about our lives for a while and we soon fell asleep it was not that rough as it was cosy.

When I woke up Victoria was up before me and was just about to go in for her morning dip. I watched her as she waved, set her clothes to one side and dived in. I shifted position to watch her and climbed down from the tree to watch her. She swam very graceful swimming. " 'bout time you woke up I'm starving!" she exclaimed. "Go find us some food if you don't mind particularly breakfast" "someone's cranky this morning" I said. "Okay, okay don't get too grouchy" I laughed. I went and looked everywhere but nothing apart from old mouldy bread that did NOT look appetising. So I came back with nothing.

By this time Victoria was dressed and looking about herself but she seems to be more successful. She had got gruel and bread from the bins so she ate that. I was cautious on what bits of it I ate which meant I had little breakfast "okay now we need to make an act to make money to have our meals and to have better clothes" " I am naturally bendy kind of depends what you need me to do. I could do splits, walkovers, walk like a crab, bend my body in half take your pick" she said. "w-w-what ?" I stammered "go begging?" I mean I don't know if this is what you do to get money. "I mean if you want I could do tumbling or I could do singing" Victoria said. "I will go look to see where we could set up and do our stunts. I will be back soon bye" she said running and doing cartwheels away "nooo wait come back!!!" I screamed still traumatised by Fred's disappearance but it was too late. She was gone now.

I sat down now on the grass waiting and waiting and waiting all over again, rocking back and forth when I heard a familiar voice yell " I"m baaaaccckkkkkk". Phew I thought all over now I breathed a sigh of relief. "There is a spot near that dough shop thingy and it's quite busy but I also got this!" she whipped out an old picnic basket and there was food in it! No not just any old gruel, an actual tuna sandwich with an apple and some bottles of juice now that was amazing.

Victoria and I feasted on it for a while then we went on a walk and we saw a big crowd of people all hunched up in a circle watching something. I squished and squirmed through them to see these middle aged men totally humiliating themselves; three of them were dancers and one was singing a rhyme that went like this

::::::How entertaining can this be:::::::::::::::::::::::::::::::::
:::::::::::::::Just look here and you will see ::::::::::::::::::::::::
:::::::::::::::::::::::: dancing about a group of three :::::::::::::
::::::::::::::::::::::::::::::::And then it is just me :::::::::::::::::::
::::::::::::::::::::::::::::::::::::: singing now before my tea :::::::::
::::::::::::::::::::::::::::::::::::::: if people give me mon-oney :

"What idiots" we both said. We went out of the road and kept walking. I saw a train station and I saw people going on and off trains every few minutes. I was amazed at this but Victoria saw me gawping and said "and said "beautiful right?" "But ain't you no chance on getting first class tickets there they cost a fortune of at least ten shillings for one ticket" "but maybe just maybe you could get one or two third class tickets for possibly 18 pennies" "how have I never heard about these!!" I said " 'cause you are a country girl" Yes that's why. "Okay we need to go and do an act, not like a show sort of act like a begging act so say that we are starving and need money to survive.

We need to go to both sides of a building and then meet back at the park when the clock tower strikes three okay" I said "okay" Victoria called and she zoomed off ahead of me she was too fast for me to catch up in my dress but we finally slowed down and chose a building that was thin and tall so I went to the left and Victoria went to the right. At first people ignored me but as soon as one coin came then they all came my pockets and my shawl were dangerously close to dropping and snapping off. As the clock struck three times I turned to the right but no one was there; I scrubbed my eyes to see if I was imagining this or not but no one was there.

I frantically started to panic but then I said to go to the park not around to the other person's side so I went to the park slowly but steadily so nothing dropped. I got to the park but no one was there but then suddenly a big head of strawberry blonde hair emerged from the bubbly water. Victoria! I ran up to her "I was looking for you everywhere I got scared when you were not at the other side of the building" "yes but I rushed to the park because I knew that is what you told me and you would be scared if you were there before me" "oh Victoria!" "How much money did you get?" I asked "I don't know, I did not count" we shared our money and sorted them into categories of different types of money and we ended up with a total of five shillings and eleven pennies "oh wow I was not expecting that on our first day!!" I said eager to go spend it but Victoria refused and said we were only going to spend three shillings of it because we still need to pay for food and we want to try and stay in a place not like a tree.

Chapter 8

We just went to get new outfits but I snuck in an extra couple pennies for any accessories so we went to this old woman's shop but she was too busy sewing to notice us in her shop. She was not anywhere near the till so people could easily steal from her but we did not dare so we asked her politely if she could help us but she pretended to ignore us but when we said we would pay good money she was all ears. She showed us her shoes and clothes and accessories and we did not actually pay good money for them but she was happy all the same. I was a bit sick of wearing dresses because you could not possibly run fast in them so I got a nice plain white blouse with little flower buttons with a short navy skirt down to my calves with white frilly socks with black old shoes. I also spotted a medium size little navy hair clip to keep your hair back from your face so I got two of these for either sides of my hair.

Victoria got the same as me apart from a navy skirt she had got a red skirt with little tiny black pearls outlining it; it was gorgeous so we happily paid delighted with our purchases and we went to a new bakery in town called Richardson's Delights. It was a lot smaller than the Dough Drop but the food was nice. I got a simple hot cross bun and it tasted very good. Victoria got a hot cross bun too. The sun was going down quicker today so we went back to the tree and slept there.

The next six months were identical to each other but it was almost our birthdays so we got excited and we wished for the days to rush by but they went by ever so slowly. It was March the twenty-fifth when we were back from eating supper that I saw a familiar face when we were walking to the park but my brain could not think of who it was. We went and rested in the tree at around seven in the evening. I was thinking about what to get her and I decided I would get her a bag like mine with her name on it. I knew it was going to be expensive but she was worth it. We went to sleep hyper for tomorrow.

I woke up at dawn and was down from the tree and left to go see where they make bags with names on it. I was walking around and around but finally I found a place that did bags but they sadly did not stitch names on but it would have to do because Victoria was an early riser and she would not like to rise and i'm not there. I purchased the bag that had red and black in it. It was spacious and pretty. I also got her a quick ready-made shawl from a stall that was tiny. It was not that good of quality but that could not be helped right now. I slipped back in unnoticed by Victoria and when she finally woke up I presented the bag and shawl to her.

She said it was amazing and that I was the best friend ever then she presented me with an even better gift : a ticket to the train station. She said it was to get to an even better surprise. The best thing about it though was that when I read the ticket it was first class! I gave Victoria a bear hug and I even went in the pond with her and I was scared because at first the water was deep and murky and cold but when I submerged in deeper I found it refreshing and Victoria taught me how to swim and I got the hang of it immediately and soon I was doing breaststroke and butterfly and front stroke and all sorts of swims. We got out of the water. We went to the train station and the station was so busy since it was a Sunday and most people travel then so we were squashed all the time we were in queue for the tickets when we tried to pay our fare the ticket man did not let us through and said we were too small to go ourselves and shooed us away. We were horrified and we went around the back and Victoria said "shhh we might get caught" so we have to go around the side and because he said we were so small we will prove to him by crawling underneath the train and hopping up in the compartment" I thought this so dangerous, sneaky and fun I dared say yes.

We snuck around to the very edge of the rails and ducked under the bush when the ticket man came near then when the train made it's tooting noise and I heard the clickety-clacking I made a run for it and jumped up at the side of the train and told Victoria to come to so she took a running jump and we got up in the compartment. We did it, we accomplished it.

We chatted to the other people in our compartment but there was this lady in our compartment darning the whole time and cracking jokes that made everyone laugh. Then it clicked she was the one I had seen when I was walking back from begging but who was she?, suddenly I realised she was the girl who was in the park last talking to Fred before his disappearance from the trip to the bathroom she must have something to do with his disappearance. I did not want to question it; looking at her face she had a lot going on behind her smile I was gazing at her when suddenly Victoria pulled me away and whispered in my ear "quick the ticket man is coming we need to go now!"

So we slipped out while the mysterious lady cracked another joke. Many of them were laughing to notice our absence. We went to go to our escape door when suddenly a guard said "what are you two up to? I have been hearing that you and you are trying to escape off this" "no, no of course not we were a...just looking for the bathroom yes" "oh okay I see well the bathroom is in the other direction" he said weirdly "well yes but we did not know that so thank you for your help and goodbye for now" and we rushed out by the guard and breathed a sigh of relief "almost got busted there" said Victoria. "Yes we have got to be more careful" I said, so we locked ourselves in the bathroom. "Do you want to know where I was taking you?" she said "yes sure, of course" I said. "Well," she said flatly "I'm taking you to the boat dock so we could go to Ireland to see your parents but that might not be possible now because the ticket person is coming around and we do not have a ticket" "well we don't have to have a ticket it would be okay to just stay in here until they come around" I said.

Just then there was a bang on the door. Then a voice said "come out here we need to check your ticket, so you come out or we come in your pick" said the voice we gulped. Then I saw a small window and I told Victoria we should escape through the window so she accepted we opened the window and Victoria climbed through but the door busted open and a woman and man came charging through and tried to grab me but when I tried to climb through the tunnel they grabbed hold of one of my ankles and they succeeded and had a firm grip but so did Victoria so she heaved one way with my arms and just about grabbed me and pulled me through but we fell the other way and bumped down a small tight hole past the window and in the compartment we were in before we plonked down perfectly beside each other and the lady cracked a joke and they laughed so once again they did not notice our arrival and continued on talking and just then the doors opened and we were there we rushed on and out of the carriage and ran past the station and out the main door and we were safe and panting for breaths we stopped and got our breaths back again and I said "I cannot believe we just done that!!!!!" "That was easily the scariest and funnest thing I've done in a while".

We started walking again and we saw a sign for the boat thing called docks so we went there and waited for a boat to come. (we had tickets for that luckily) so we went there and got our tickets approved and got on "the boat is not properly fully boarded yet so we should get comfy" I told Victoria we had our own compartment in the boat because it was first class so that time flew by and we were soon in Ireland we ate one or two buns in our compartment and then we were allowed to leave in fifteen minutes after the boat properly is secured and fasten with an anchor so we waited those minutes and stepped out safely with the guidance of the ship driver.

When we got down I asked where we were to the man in front of us, by the way he was acting I think he was from Ireland and was Irish he replied with "why you are in Dublin now wee lassie why? Are you travelling somewhere where is it I can give you directions?" "well we are trying to get to Wicklow if you know where that is?" I asked politely. "That's a right wee travel then if you are going by foot it would take you at least five days or so just keep going straight that's all I can give lassie bye fer now" and he rushed off and we set off happily on our journey to Wicklow hand in hand me and Victoria were off together happily ever after.

THE END

Printed in Great Britain
by Amazon